Albert
EINSTEIN

Saviour Pirotta

HODDER
Wayland

an imprint of Hodder Children's Books

© 2001 White-Thomson Publishing Ltd

Produced for Hodder Wayland by
White-Thomson Publishing Ltd
2/3 St Andrew's Place
Lewes
BN7 1UP

Editor: Polly Goodman
Designer: Derek Lee
Picture Researcher: Shelley Noronha, Glass Onion Pictures
Cover and Title Page Illustrator: Richard Hook
Science Panel Illustrator: Derek Lee
Map Illustrator: Tim Mayer
Consultant: Dr Brian Bowers, Senior Research Fellow at the Science
    Museum, London.
Proofreader: Katie Orchard

Published in Great Britain in 2001 by Hodder Wayland,
an imprint of Hodder Children's Books.
This paperback edition published in 2002
The right of Saviour Pirotta to be identified as the author of this
work has been asserted by him in accordance with the Copyright,
Designs and Patents Act 1988.

British Library Cataloguing in Publication Data
Pirotta, Saviour, 1958 –
Albert Einstein. – (Scientists Who Made History)
1. Einstein, Albert, 1879-1955
2. Physicists – Germany
I. Title
530'.092

ISBN 0750238879

Printed and bound in Italy by G. Canale & C.S.p.A, Turin

Hodder Children's Books
A division of Hodder Headline Limited
338 Euston Road, London, NW1 3BH

Picture Acknowledgements: AKG 5, 9b, 14, 19t, 20, 21, 22, 24, 28, 30,
33t, 34, 39; Corbis 4, 7t, 13, 16, 25, 36, 37b, 38, 43t, 43b; Mary
Evans 11, 31, 37t; Hodder Wayland Picture Library 7b, 8, 9t, 10, 15,
18, 19b, 32, 33b; Peter Newark 40, 41; Popperfoto 27, 42; Ann
Ronan Picture Library 6, 23, 35; Topham 12, 17, 26, 29.

Contents

Revolution in Science

ON SUNDAY 29 May 1919, there was a total eclipse of the Sun. It was only visible from a few places around the world. One of them was Principe, an island off the west coast of Africa. As the Moon blotted out the Sun, an English astronomer called Arthur Eddington took photographs of the darkened sky from the island. Later, Eddington compared the photographs with pictures taken six months earlier, when the Sun was on the other side of the world. Both sets of photographs showed the same piece of sky. But in the second batch taken during the eclipse, the stars seemed to have moved slightly.

BELOW: *The English astronomer Sir Arthur Stanley Eddington (left) was born in 1882. A noted astronomer and physicist, he did research on stars and why they shine. Here he is pictured with a colleague at an astronomer's conference in 1921. He died in 1944.*

RELATIVITY

The theory of relativity is based on the simple idea that everything is relative to everything else. When you are doing something exciting, time seems to pass quickly. An hour can feel more like a few minutes. But when you are doing something boring, time seems to drag. One hour can feel more like two or three. That's because you are measuring time from a different perspective. Everything is relative. Einstein applied the idea to measuring time, motion, speed, mass and gravity.

Such a small difference between the pictures would not have meant anything to an ordinary photographer. But on 6 November 1919, Eddington showed both sets of photographs to members of the Royal Society and the Royal Astronomical Society in London. He explained that the stars in the photos were really beams of light projected by distant suns. In the first batch of photos, the beams were travelling towards the Earth through empty space. But in the pictures taken during the eclipse, the beams of light had been bent by the Sun's gravity, making the stars look as if they had shifted position.

The members of the Royal Societies were impressed. Eddington's photographs proved that a complex theory about the relationship between mass, gravity and speed was correct. Called the general theory of relativity, it was the work of a German scientist by the name of Albert Einstein. His theory called into question everything scientists believed about the way in which the universe worked.

Eddington's announcement took the world by storm. The next day articles with sensational headlines like 'Revolution In Science', 'Lights All Askew In The Heavens' and 'Space Warped' appeared in the papers. Albert Einstein became a household name. Even though most people had no idea what the theory of relativity meant, the public wanted to know more about this obscure scientist, who was being called 'a genius'. Einstein's every move was reported on by journalists. People wanted his opinion on every subject under the sun.

IN THEIR OWN WORDS

'*When you sit with a nice girl for two hours, it seems like two minutes. When you sit on a hot stove for two minutes, it seems like two hours. That's relativity.*'

EINSTEIN EXPLAINING THE CONCEPT OF RELATIVITY.

PHYSICS IN THE NINETEENTH CENTURY

Towards the second half of the nineteenth century, scientists were making groundbreaking discoveries, and one of the hottest subjects was the establishment of electrical science. In 1831, the English scientist Michael Faraday discovered a way to generate electricity by machine rather than from chemical cells. It was the beginning of the modern age, affecting the lives of millions. In 1864, another scientist, called James Clerk Maxwell, published his theory showing how light consists of waves of electric and magnetic forces, called electromagnetic waves. His work led to the discovery of radio waves.

LEFT: *Michael Faraday was born in London in 1791. He started working as a bookbinder at the age of thirteen and in 1813, he became an assistant to the famous chemist Sir Humphry Davy. Faraday achieved his discoveries about electricity through a mixture of painstaking research and gut instinct.*

LEFT: *The German scientist Wilhelm Conrad Röntgen (1845–1923) won the Nobel Prize for Physics in 1901 for his discovery of X-rays. His contribution to science has helped millions of people around the world.*

On 8 November 1895, the German scientist Wilhelm Röntgen discovered X-rays. These are electrical charges that pass easily through some materials, but not others. One of the materials they cannot pass through is bone. Wilhelm printed an X-ray of his wife's hand, showing the bones and a ring, but not the flesh and blood. Soon, other scientists had modified the idea to use X-rays in hospitals, to help identify broken bones and to study the digestive system.

In 1898, the Polish scientist Marie Curie and her French husband Pierre studied uranium ore and discovered two highly radioactive elements within it. They named these elements radium and polonium. In 1903, the Curies won the Nobel Prize for Physics for their work on uranium and radioactivity. In 1911, Marie went on to win the Nobel Prize for Chemistry for her work on radium. During the First World War, Marie Curie showed how X-rays could locate bullets inside the human body. She also invented special vehicles to carry X-ray equipment out to wounded French soldiers on the battlefields, and trained people how to use them.

When Einstein's general theory of relativity became public in 1919, to many people it seemed that he had become successful overnight. In fact, the humble scientist had been working away at his various groundbreaking theories for many years. His journey to fame and fortune started in Ulm, a city in Germany…

BELOW: *Marie Curie (1867–1934) was born in Warsaw, Poland, but spent most of her life in Paris. After winning the Nobel Prize for Chemistry in 1911, she became the only person to win two Nobels. This photograph was taken in about 1906, when she became the first female professor at the Sorbonne, the University of Paris.*

Early Years

ALBERT EINSTEIN WAS born to middle-class Jewish parents in Ulm, Germany on 14 March 1879. When his mother Pauline saw him for the first time, she was worried that he might be deformed because he had such a big head. His grandmother declared him 'too fat'.

Albert lived in Ulm, a city on the left bank of the Danube river, for the first year of his life. Then, some time in 1880, his family moved to Munich. There Albert's father Hermann planned to set up an electrical engineering and plumbing business with his brother Jakob. Hermann was not very good at business and his family was often short of money. He hoped that by teaming up with his brother, he could make some money. Many people in Germany were starting to use electricity and Hermann hoped to sell them his electrical goods.

ABOVE: *Einstein's father Hermann was very good at mathematics and excelled at school. But as an adult, he found it difficult to say 'no' to business partners and this trait caused his family financial hardship.*

BELOW AND LEFT: *These maps show where Einstein spent most of his life, first in Germany and Switzerland (below), and later in the USA (left).*

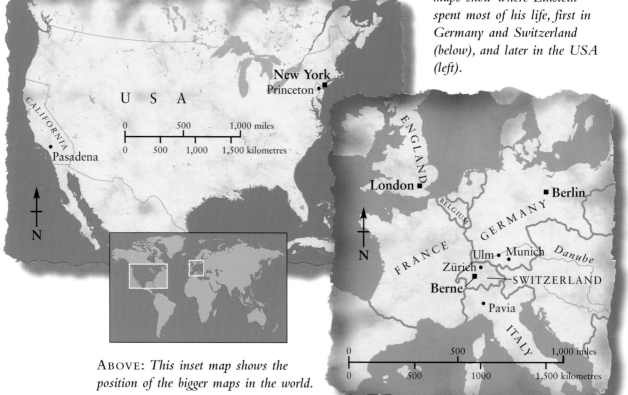

ABOVE: *This inset map shows the position of the bigger maps in the world.*

LEFT: *Einstein's mother Pauline was very cultured and encouraged her children to study music. One of her greatest passions was reading.*

'Where are the wheels?'

EINSTEIN AGED TWO, ON SEEING HIS NEW BABY SISTER MAJA FOR THE FIRST TIME.

'His face would turn completely yellow, the tip of his nose snow white, and he was no longer in control of himself.'

MAJA, DESCRIBING EINSTEIN'S TANTRUMS WHEN HE WAS A CHILD.

According to his family, Albert was a rather shy infant who did not seem to need much looking after. When he began to talk, at about the age of two, he did not use baby language like other children of his age. Instead, he would make up proper sentences in his head before saying anything. Albert's relatives would often see him struggling to string the words together, frowning with concentration.

When Albert was two, his baby sister Maja was born. As toddlers, Albert and Maja got on well, but Einstein had a terrible habit of throwing toys at her head. Once, while she was playing quietly, he even hit her on the head with a garden hoe.

As a toddler, Albert didn't like playing with other children, preferring to amuse himself with his own toys. He often lost his temper, especially when anyone tried to stop him playing. This led many people to believe that he was difficult and rather stupid. How wrong they were!

RIGHT: *Albert aged four years old, posing for a photograph in 1883.*

SCHOOL DAYS

In early 1884, when Albert was five years old, his parents enrolled him at the Volksschule, a Catholic Elementary School close to where they lived. The teachers at the Volksschule were very strict. Pupils were expected to obey the rules and to learn a lot of things by heart. Most important of all, they were expected to accept everything their teachers told them. Those who disobeyed, got behind in their schoolwork, or failed to remember their multiplication tables were severely punished. Teachers took great delight in rapping students' knuckles with a cane.

BELOW: *Einstein's sister was born in 1881. Her name was Maria, but everyone called her Maja. During their childhood, Albert and Maja were very close, and they remained friends throughout their lives.*

Albert, who loved solving mathematical problems his own way, was often given such punishments. He also found it difficult to fit in with the other pupils, preferring to read on his own. On many occasions, Albert's teachers complained to the headmaster that he was slow in learning things and held up all the other children.

At home, though, things were different. Albert would spend many happy hours constructing models and playing with a set of building blocks. His powers of concentration were very strong and his parents would often notice that he never gave up on a puzzle until he had solved it. None of this impressed his teachers at the Volkscchule, however, even though he did manage to get good reports. When Albert's father once asked the headmaster how his son was doing, the headmaster sniffed haughtily and said: 'Nothing will ever become of Master Albert.'

The Needle in the Compass

One day, when Albert was still only five, he was ill in bed when his father gave him a compass to play with. Albert could not understand why the needle always pointed north, no matter which way he turned the instrument. He became fascinated by the fact that the needle was obeying an invisible force outside the compass. What could this powerful force be, he wondered? Where was it hidden? Why couldn't he see it? Albert was determined to find out for himself. He spent a lot of time thinking about the problem, trying to solve it in his mind.

BELOW: *A French classroom in 1889. The younger children on the back row are using chalkboards, while the older children in front use pens dipped in inkwells on their desks.*

IN THEIR OWN WORDS

'That this needle behaved in such a determined way did not at all fit into the kind of occurrences that could find a place in the unconscious world of concepts. I can still remember – or at least believe I can remember – that this experience made a deep and lasting impression upon me.'

ALBERT EINSTEIN RECALLING THE DAY HE WAS GIVEN A COMPASS TO PLAY WITH, PUBLISHED IN *AUTOBIOGRAPHICAL NOTES*, 1949.

MATHEMATICS

In 1889, aged ten years old, Albert left the Volksschule and started attending another school called the Luitpold Gymnasium. At first, his school reports were very good, but soon his grades started to slip. His teachers, who always followed their lesson plans very carefully, were baffled and often irritated by this big-headed student who insisted on learning things his own way. Before long they had labelled him a time-waster. There was only one teacher in the whole school who recognized Albert's gift for original thought and encouraged him to work on his own. His name was Herr Reuss.

BELOW: *A photograph of Einstein aged fourteen. In his early teens, Einstein became interested in philosophy, an interest that stayed with him all his life. His scientific works make many references to philosophical thoughts and ideas.*

IN THEIR OWN WORDS

'Imagination is more important than knowledge. Education is what remains after one has forgotten everything he learned in school. The important thing is not to stop questioning. The only thing that interferes with my learning is my education.'

SOME OF EINSTEIN'S REVOLUTIONARY THOUGHTS ABOUT EDUCATION.

Gradually, Albert realized that if he was to get the education he wanted, he was going to have to study on his own. His uncle encouraged him by giving him a book about algebra. Albert took to the subject like a duck to water and when he was twelve, he decided to study advanced algebra. Albert's uncle was very impressed by the way he searched for an answer to every problem that he was set. At last Albert had found a subject to which he could dedicate all his free time: mathematics.

The Influence of Max Talmud

When Albert was ten, he was introduced to Max Talmud, a medical student who used to come to dinner at the Einsteins' every Thursday. At the time, many well-off Jewish families used to help poor Jewish students in any way they could. In return for the Einsteins' hospitality, Talmud would lend Albert his favourite science books.

Albert liked Max right away. The young student treated Albert as an equal and would discuss many scientific ideas and theories with him, ideas in which his teachers at the Luitpold were not remotely interested. Talmud introduced the eager Albert to many important textbooks of the day, including Spieker's *Lehrbuch der ebenen Geometrie* (Textbook of Levels of Geometry). When he was older, Einstein would claim that this book was the main reason why he became obsessed with mathematics. Talmud also lent Albert a copy of Immanuel Kant's *Critique of Pure Reason*. This was a book of philosophy and Albert was immediately intrigued by the subject.

ABOVE: *The German philosopher Immanuel Kant (1724–1804). His book* Critique of Pure Reason *remained a major influence on philosophers and students for a long time. Published in 1781, it was regarded as a work that sought to determine the limits of man's knowledge. Another work,* Critique of Practical Reason, *appeared in 1788.*

ABOVE: *New recruits stand to attention in Berlin, in 1908. Einstein found the idea of being a soldier highly disturbing. Once, when his father took him to see a parade, he burst into tears and covered his face with his hands. In his teens, he refused to do military duty and, as an adult, took every opportunity to condemn violence.*

EINSTEIN AND RELIGION

At the age of twelve, Albert became interested in Judaism. He gave up non-kosher food and started reading the Bible. When he was thirteen, however, Albert decided that what he was reading clashed with the knowledge he was gaining from his scientific studies. He turned away from religion, saying it was being used by governments to prevent ordinary people from thinking for themselves. He also became a pacifist, a person who hates war and violence. At school, Albert forced himself to question everything he heard from his teachers and to look at everything from a new angle. Albert Einstein was starting to think like a scientist.

Expulsion

In 1894, when Albert was fifteen, his parents moved again, this time to Pavia in Italy. They left Albert behind in Munich, so he could do his exams at the Luitpold Gymnasium. He lived in a boarding house, where he could study algebra and geometry to his heart's content. But the situation at school was becoming unbearable to Albert. He found the lessons becoming more boring by the day. To make matters worse, he realized that after his exams, he would have to do military duty. At the time, all young German men aged seventeen were forced to join the army for a year.

As a pacifist, Einstein was opposed to being a soldier, and he thought that the army officers would be even stricter than the teachers at the Gymnasium. So, he got himself expelled from the school and in the spring of 1895, joined his family in Italy.

At this point in his life, Einstein had no idea how he wanted to earn his living, but he thought about becoming a teacher. His father insisted that he went to university to get a degree. So Albert was sent to Zurich in Switzerland, to do a science course at the Federal Institute of Technology.

'If I were to have the good fortune to pass my exams I would go to Zurich. I would stay there for four years in order to study mathematics and physics. I imagine myself becoming a teacher in those branches of the natural sciences.'

EINSTEIN, IN A SHORT FRENCH ESSAY HE WROTE BEFORE GOING TO ZURICH IN 1896.

RIGHT: *Before enrolling at the Federal Institute of Technology in Zurich, Einstein spent some time studying in a Swiss school in Aarau, some 32 kilometres outside Zurich. It was the first school in which he really felt at home. Here he is pictured (far left, seated) with his fellow students.*

Work and Studies

TYPICALLY, EINSTEIN ATTENDED only the lectures he was interested in at the Federal Institute. Most of his time was spent in cafés and restaurants, where he kept his friends fascinated with his talk of physics. One of the five students on his course was a young woman called Mileva Maric. Einstein fell in love with her and the pair spent a lot of time relaxing instead of studying. No wonder that at the end of the three-year course in June 1900, Einstein graduated with lower grades than expected, and Mileva failed her exams.

Saddled with poor qualifications and a reputation for being scornful of authority, Einstein could not get a job at the Federal Institute. Instead he had to accept a job at the Swiss Patent Office in Berne. Everyone thought that Einstein had missed his chance to make his mark on the world of science. In fact, he had found a job that left him a lot of free time in which to work on his mathematical theories.

BELOW: *Many academics considered the Federal Institute of Technology in Zurich one of the best colleges in Europe. It had an extensive physics department and a large laboratory, which was well-stocked with equipment. This photograph was taken in about 1900.*

The Behaviour of Molecules

While working at the Patent Office, Einstein planned to
write a thesis that would earn him a Ph.D. from the
University of Zurich. This qualification would get him a
job as a university researcher, where he would have access
to all the books he needed for his personal studies. It
would also gain him a foothold on the academic ladder.

Einstein started working at the Patent Office in June
1902. Six months later, on 6 January 1903, he married
Mileva. In his spare time, Einstein wrote several papers,
mostly dealing with the behaviour of molecules. At this
time, many scientists doubted their very existence. For
his thesis, Einstein made calculations that described
the behaviour of molecules in liquid. He based his
observations on the way sugar dissolved in hot tea.
He even found out that a sugar molecule measured
one-millionth of a centimetre across.

BELOW: *Young Einstein's wit, his
ability to play the violin and the piano,
and his reputation as a rebel all helped
to make him the centre of attention in
any crowd. Girls also loved his wavy
black hair and moustache. Here he is
aged twenty-one.*

IN THEIR OWN WORDS

'What really
interests me is
whether God had
any choice in the
creation of the world.'

EINSTEIN'S VIEWS ON GOD AND RELIGION OFTEN
CLASHED WITH THOSE OF OTHERS.

FIRST PUBLICATIONS

Einstein's thesis was finished in April 1905 and he presented it to the University of Zurich in July. The professors were very impressed by it but they had one objection: it wasn't long enough to merit a Ph.D. Legend has it that an angry Einstein added just one sentence and presented it again. This time he was awarded the Ph.D. right away. With several published papers and a Ph.D. under his belt, Einstein was at last making his mark on the scientific community in Europe.

BELOW: *For many years, Albert and Mileva were inseparable. A Serbian, Mileva had a passion for social justice and the causes of racial minorities. She was also a good mathematician and physicist, and helped Einstein with his work by checking his arithmetic.*

The Photoelectric Effect

The year 1905 was a busy one for Einstein. Not only did he finish and present his thesis, he also had three papers published in the German science journal *Annalen der Physik* (Annals of Physics). One of these papers dealt with the photoelectric effect and was later to win him the Nobel Prize for Physics. Many scientists before Einstein believed that light travelled only in waves, like water rippling across a pond. Einstein suggested that light contained particles, later called photons. The brighter the light, the more photons it contained.

At the time, no-one took Einstein's paper on the photoelectric effect very seriously. One American physicist, Robert Millikan, even set up some experiments to prove Einstein wrong. But he couldn't. The more Millikan experimented, the more he became convinced that Einstein was right. And in 1923, Millikan was awarded the Nobel Prize for Physics himself, partly for the work he did on Einstein's theory.

ABOVE: *Einstein's wooden desk at the Swiss Patent Office was the perfect place to develop his various theories. He used to hide his papers in a drawer when anyone came into the room unannounced.*

BELOW: *Einstein's illustration of the Brownian motion, showing the path followed by a particle suspended in liquid. The many sudden turns are caused by the impact of the molecules in the liquid.*

BROWNIAN MOTION

Einstein's third paper for the *Annalen der Physik* in 1905 explained the Brownian motion, where particles seen in light move in a zigzag pattern, like dust particles seen in a beam of sunlight. Einstein used mathematical calculations to prove that sometimes the particles were hit by others more on one side than the other, which made them zigzag.

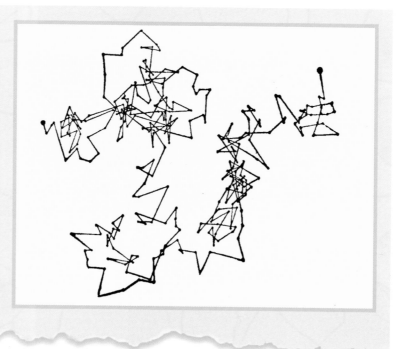

THEORY OF RELATIVITY

BELOW: *This photographic image illustrates Einstein's theory of relativity concerning the constancy of the speed of light. Einstein later said that the theory grew out of his desire to improve the foundations of physics as it existed at the turn of the twentieth century.*

On 30 June 1905, the editors of the *Annalen der Physik* received a third paper from Einstein. It was his famous theory of relativity, which the journal published in September of that year. This paper explained the behaviour of light and moving objects.

Einstein believed that the speed of light was the same however it was measured. But if space and time were measured together, the result would depend on where you were and how fast or slow you were moving. So, a clock on a spaceship ticked slower than an identical one sitting on a table on Earth.

As soon as he sent in his paper, Einstein realized that his calculations proved that mass and energy were related. He wrote a second article, published in November 1905, which included the most famous formula in physics the world has ever seen: $E=Mc^2$. This means 'energy equals mass times the velocity of light squared', where 'E' stands for energy, 'M' stands for mass and 'c' stands for the velocity of light. The formula meant that a small amount of matter could be turned into a lot of powerful energy. Later in the twentieth century, this knowledge would be used to create nuclear energy and the atom bomb.

Einstein's theory of relativity did not catch scientists' imagination right away. Up until then, everyone had believed that time was measured in the same way all around the universe. Back in the seventeenth century, the British scientist Sir Isaac

Newton had explained how time marched on at the same pace in every corner of the universe. Now here was another scientist trying to prove otherwise. To make matters worse, many scientists could not get to grips with the complex equations they needed to solve before they could understand Einstein's theory.

BELOW: *Part of Einstein's hand-written manuscript on his 'general' theory of relativity, the successor to his first 'special' theory. In 1944, one of Einstein's own copies of the 'special' theory was auctioned in America for US$6 million. It can now be found in the Library of Congress.*

THE BEHAVIOUR OF MUONS

Einstein's theory that time moves slower for objects travelling at a fast speed has been proved time and time again. High in the world's atmosphere there are particles called muons, which are created by cosmic rays hitting the atmosphere and only lasting for two microseconds. There should not be enough time for them to reach the ground. But scientists have discovered that they do reach the Earth. One explanation is that muons travel so fast that their two microseconds last for much longer.

Lecturer and Professor

THE FIRST YEARS of their marriage were very happy
ones for Albert and Mileva Einstein. In 1904, their son Hans
Albert was born. Einstein was given a bigger salary and
immediately took up sailing, a hobby he was to stay
interested in for the rest of his life. Two years later he was
promoted to the post of Technical Expert at the Patent
Office. The extra money from the promotion meant the
Einsteins could at last have a decent quality of life.

In his spare time, Einstein
continued his research. His work was
now attracting a lot of attention and
several people encouraged him to
find academic work. In 1907,
Einstein applied to be a *privatdozent*,
or part-time lecturer, at the
University of Berne. *Privatdozents*
were not paid salaries. They were
expected to live off the money
students paid for one-off lectures. But
it was considered the first step
towards a full-time post in education.
Einstein included a copy of his
theory of relativity with his
application for the job. The professors
couldn't understand it, so they
refused him the job. Disheartened
but not defeated, Einstein continued
to work at the Patent Office while
applying for more posts. Time and
time again, he was unsuccessful. At
last, in 1908, the University of Berne
changed its mind and offered him
the post of *privatdozent*.

BELOW: *The birth of Albert
and Mileva's first son
Hans Albert, in 1904, brought
much joy to his parents. The
family lived in a well-furnished
top-floor flat, paid for by
Einstein's modest salary at the
Patent Office.*

Delighted, Einstein started his academic career in September 1908, at the age of twenty-nine. Since he had to fit the lectures around his work at the Patent Office, he could only teach early in the morning or on Saturdays. These were unpopular times for the students, so very few of them turned up to listen to his talks, which began explaining the theory of radiation. Sometimes he found himself lecturing to his friends, or to his younger sister Maja, who was taking a language course at the university.

IN THEIR OWN WORDS

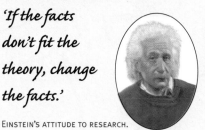

'If the facts don't fit the theory, change the facts.'

EINSTEIN'S ATTITUDE TO RESEARCH.

LEFT: *Einstein chose the theory of radiation as the subject for his first lecture as a* privatdozent *at the University of Berne. Only four students attended the course, but things were soon to change for the young scientist.*

'The views of space and time which I wish to lay before you have sprung from the soil of experimental physics, and therein lies their strength. They are radical. Henceforth space by itself, and time by itself, are destined to fade away into mere shadows, and only a kind of union of the two will preserve an independent reality.'

HERMANN MINKOWSKI IN HIS FAMOUS LECTURE
AT COLOGNE, ON 2 SEPTEMBER 1908.

BELOW: *Hermann Minkowski was born in Russia in 1864. He won the coveted Paris Prize for Mathematics in 1882 and went on to have a dazzling career. His collaboration with Einstein continued until he died in 1909.*

EINSTEIN EXPLAINED

Einstein's lack of an audience soon changed. Help was to come from Hermann Minkowski, one of his old enemies at the Institute in Zurich. Minkowski had been one of Einstein's teachers at the Institute. He had once described Einstein as 'a lazy dog that never bothered about mathematics.' Faced with the brilliance of his ex-pupil's theory, Minkowski now had to change his mind. He added images to Einstein's mathematical calculations to help people understand his theories.

In a lecture given in Cologne, on 2 September 1908, Minkowski presented Einstein's theory of relativity, adding his own interpretation with the use of images. His audience listened open-mouthed as he explained how, by fusing the ideas of space and time, Einstein had discovered a fourth dimension: space-time.

At first Einstein did not like Minkowski's interpretation of his work. But since it helped to spread his ideas among the European scientific community, he grew to like it. He even worked with Minkowski on the theory, until Minkowski died suddenly in 1909.

Scientific Acclaim

Hermann Minkowski's paper explaining Einstein's theory of relativity was published to great acclaim shortly after his death in 1909. Partly as a result of it, Einstein was offered the post of Professor of Physics at the University of Zurich. At last he had an academic job that earned him a proper salary. It was only the first in a series of appointments that were offered to him. In 1911, he was lured to the German University of Prague, where he was appointed chair (head) of theoretical physics. A year later he returned to Zurich, to teach at his former Institute of Technology. By now, offers of work were flooding in from various institutions around Europe. Everyone, it seemed, wanted the famous physicist working for them.

In 1913, at the age of thirty-four, Einstein was given the best offer yet: a professorship at the University of Berlin. The post offered a very good salary and, most important of all, a lot of time for scientific work and research. After some deliberation, Einstein agreed and the family moved to Germany so that Albert could start work in April 1914.

BELOW: *Einstein (second from right, standing) and scientist Marie Curie (second from right, sitting) attend a special conference of famous scientists in Brussels, in October 1911.*

ABOVE: *Mileva often had to look after Hans Albert and Eduard on her own. Although he loved his children, Einstein was not a family man. His main priority was his work. It is said that Mileva resented the fact that, because of Einstein's fame, she had to give up her own studies and ambitions.*

IN THEIR OWN WORDS

'I was sitting in a chair at the Patent Office at Berne when all of a sudden a thought occurred to me: 'If a person falls freely he will not feel his own weight.' I was startled. This simple thought made a deep impression on me. It impelled me toward a theory of gravitation.'

EINSTEIN DESCRIBES THE MOMENT HE STARTED WORKING ON THE GENERAL THEORY OF RELATIVITY.

Mileva did not like Berlin at all. Shortly after Einstein started work at the university, she returned to Switzerland, taking the children with her. By now the Einsteins had a second child, a son called Eduard, who was born in 1910. Einstein was left alone to continue his work. He was looked after by his cousin Elsa, who happened to live nearby with her children. Einstein needed looking after, too. He was working night and day, extending his theory of relativity to include gravity and acceleration.

Gravity and Acceleration

Einstein had first started thinking about gravity and acceleration back in 1907, while he was still working at the Swiss Patent Office. He had a brilliant idea that he later referred to as, 'the happiest thought of my life.' It occurred to him that if someone fell off a building, they would not feel the effect of gravity. They would merely feel as if they were floating, like an astronaut in space. By using thought experiments, Einstein concluded that acceleration cancels out gravity.

In 1911, Einstein had started working on the theory of relativity again. For the next four years he polished his ideas about gravity and acceleration, fitting the work round other jobs. By the end of the process, Einstein had predicted that space was curved, and that objects travelling through space curved with it. He believed that space bent to accommodate objects like planets, and that matter travelling through space curved with it.

Einstein had created his masterpiece, which became known as the general theory of relativity. In November 1915, he presented his theory to the Prussian Academy of Science. But many scientists found it very difficult to accept that space could be curved. According to Sir Isaac Newton, it was an unchanging place, a blank backdrop against which all planets moved.

There was a way in which Einstein's theory could be proved, by taking pictures of the dark sky before and after a total eclipse. If Einstein was right, the invisible Sun in the picture of an eclipse would force the starlight to bend. The stars would show up in slightly different positions between the two photographs. In 1914, an expedition headed by the astronomer Erwin Finlay-Freundlich set off to southern Russia to take the photographs. But its efforts were thwarted by the First World War.

ABOVE: *A German machine-gun section in Poland during the First World War.*

BENDING THE LIGHT

The best way to understand the idea of light 'bending' in space is to imagine that space is a stretched rubber sheet and a beam of light is a marble. If you rolled the marble across the rubber sheet, it would move in a straight line. If you put a heavy ball (representing the Sun) on the sheet, the rubber would bend under its weight. Now if you rolled the marble across the sheet again, it would travel around the dent caused by the ball. This is how light travels around the Sun.

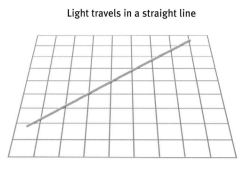

Light travels in a straight line

Light bends around the Sun

WAR AND DIVORCE

Einstein was very disappointed that the expedition to Russia had failed. He had always hated war, particularly the way that soldiers were expected to obey orders without thinking for themselves. He felt that this robbed them of their individuality. Most of all, Einstein detested the fact that fighting disrupted co-operation between scientists from different countries working towards a common goal.

Not all scientists in Germany agreed with Einstein's pacifist beliefs, however. Most of them supported their government's decision to go to war. Some even helped develop war machinery and weapons. Einstein was appalled to discover that intelligent human beings would willingly use science to harm other people.

BELOW: *German soldiers march across Berlin in 1914, the same year that Einstein came to live in the city. The scientist found the anti-Semitic feeling in Germany very disturbing. His attempts to denounce war and weaponry marked him out as a pacifist.*

When, in October 1914, fellow intellectuals in Germany signed a manifesto saying that they agreed with their government's attack on nearby nations, Einstein immediately signed a counter-manifesto. Unfortunately, only three other people signed it. The German authorities were relieved. The failure of Einstein's counter-manifesto showed that despite his reputation within the scientific community, Einstein did not have much influence on European society at large.

Cousin Elsa

Meanwhile, there was trouble on the Einstein home front too. Albert and Mileva were growing apart. Perhaps Mileva, a scientist herself, resented being pushed into the background while her husband grew more important. Since Mileva had moved back to Switzerland, the distance between them did not make matters any easier. Influenced by his mother, Hans Albert stopped writing to his father. Then, in 1917, Einstein fell ill with various complaints, including a stomach ulcer and jaundice. Unable to work fine-tuning his general theory of relativity, he became depressed.

Luckily, Einstein's cousin, Elsa, was still looking after him. She fed him hot meals, made from the meagre ingredients she could buy in war-torn Berlin. As Einstein's health improved, his friendship with Elsa developed into love. He asked Mileva for a divorce and she agreed – on one condition. If Einstein ever won the Nobel Prize, he was to give her the prize money. Einstein, not bothered about finances, agreed. In February 1919, he was divorced from Mileva. He and Elsa were married in June 1919, less than a year after the First World War had ended.

ABOVE: *Elsa Lowenthal and her cousin Albert had played together as children. With Einstein divorced and Elsa a widow, they were the perfect match. The new Mrs Einstein had no particular interest in science, but she and Albert were married in 1919.*

IN THEIR OWN WORDS

'He who joyfully marches to music in rank and file has already earned my contempt. He has been given a large brain by mistake, since for him the spinal cord would fully suffice.'

EINSTEIN EXPRESSES HIS OPINION OF THE ARMY.

Fame and Glory

THE SECOND ATTEMPT to prove Einstein's general theory by taking pictures of the stars was successful. In November 1919, its results were shown to members of the Royal Society and the Royal Astronomical Society during a special meeting in London (see pages 4–5). As a result, the general public wanted to know what the theory of relativity meant. Few could understand it but, in a Europe still feeling the after-effects of war, many people were more than willing to turn away from the destruction around them and look to the stars for new hope.

Einstein was besieged with requests to give interviews. He sold hundreds of pictures of himself to magazines and papers. The profits were given to a children's charity in Austria. To help people understand the theory of relativity, Einstein wrote his own article for the *Times* newspaper. The public read it with interest.

BELOW: *By 1921, Einstein had become one of the most famous scientists in the world. Pictures like this one, taken in his study, appeared in papers, books and magazines all over the world. Albert viewed his new-found fame with scepticism. Elsa often had to protect him from insistent journalists and photographers.*

Nicht wegwerfen!   Weitergeben!

Die Totengräber Rußlands

Lenin (richtiger Name Uljanow). Der Russe Uljanow war allerdings der Stiefvater Lenins. Lenin hatte eine Jüdin zur Frau, die Kinder lernen hebräisch. Lenin hat den Sonntag in Rußland abgeschafft und den jüd. Sabatt als Feiertag eingeführt. Er hat die Kirchen in Kinos und Tanzsäle verwandelt, während die Synagogen unberührt blieben und die jüdischen Rabbiner nach wie vor ihr Amt ausüben.

Der Jude Trotzky (richtiger Name Braunstein), wurde 1917 auf Vorstellungen der Juden hin in Frankreich aus der Haft entlassen, in New York mit Geld ausgestattet, und auf das russische Volk losgelassen.

Der Jude Jankel Jurowsky, Mörder des Zaren und Familie.

Der Jude Sinowjew (richtiger Name Apfelbaum). Der Massenschlächter von Moskau.

Der Jude K. Radek (richtiger Name Sobelsohn), später Sowjetagent in Berlin gewesen.

Der Jude Swerdlow II. Vors. des 4. Kongresses d. Arbeiter- u. Soldatenräte.

Der Jude Moses Uritzky, Kommissar z. Bekämpfung d. Gegenrevolution (Tscheka). Massenmörder.

Der Jude Efremow-Chaimoritsch, Leiter der politischen Abteilung der X. Armee.

Der Jude Stecklow (richtiger Name Nachamkes). Pressediktator der Sowjet-Regierung.

Der Jude Schreider (im Kommissariat für d. Innere)

Der Jude Awancsow, Sekretär des Vollzugsrates.

Der Jude Martow (richtiger Name Zederbaum). Mitglied der Exekutive der Arbeiterräte.

Der Jude Samuel Berkmann, Moskauer Agent in Amerika.

Der Jude Wolodarsky (richtiger Name Cohen). Mitglied des Vollzugsrates.

Soon, more than a hundred books about Einstein's theory of relativity had flooded the market. Thousands of articles, features and even cartoons appeared in the papers. After years of hard work and research, Albert Einstein had become the symbol of modern science.

However, not everyone accepted the theory of relativity. Some journalists heaped scorn on an idea that could not be proved in a way they could see with their own eyes. Other physicists, jealous of Einstein's success, claimed that his theory went against common sense. Everyone could see with their own eyes that space was flat and not curved. But the most dangerous critics of Einstein's achievements were German politicians. They detested Einstein, not because he was a threat to established ideas, but because he was Jewish.

ABOVE: *The Nazi Party's propaganda machine always ridiculed Jewish people. In this leaflet, it accuses Jews of destroying Russia and making it a haven for Communists. Only Adolf Hitler, the leaflet insists, can save Germany from ruin.*

EINSTEIN THE ACTIVIST

Since his brief interest in religion as a teenager, Einstein had never really thought about the fact that he was Jewish. For him, all people were the same, no matter what faith they held or what country they were born in. But, as the Germans started to blame the Jews for their downfall in the First World War, he felt he had to do something to help fellow Jewish scientists who were being refused work in universities.

In 1920, Einstein joined the Zionist movement, a group of people who believed that Jews should have their own homeland in Palestine. Einstein did not believe that this was possible, but he was attracted to the idea of a Hebrew University, where Jews could work without fear of harassment. A few months later, he went on a fund-raising tour of the USA, accompanied by his friend and leader of the Zionist movement, Chaim Weizmann.

ABOVE: *Elsa and Albert, (second and third from the right) arrive in the USA aboard the SS* Rotterdam. *With them are (from the left) Dr Mendel Ussishkim, a Russian Zionist leader, Professor Chaim Weizmann and his wife, and Dr Ben Zion Mosensohn, a professor at the Hebrew High School of Jaffe, in Palestine.*

LEFT: *Crowds cheer Einstein on the streets of New York City. During his speeches in the USA, Einstein talked about the need for setting up a Hebrew University. A large amount of money was raised for the project.*

BELOW: *Einstein talks to people on the steps of City Hall, New York City, on 17 May 1921. The crowds, fascinated by his theories and his fame, listened patiently. Local papers published all the details of his visit.*

Enormous crowds greeted Einstein as his ship docked in New York Harbour. Newspaper photographers clambered aboard to take pictures of him and Elsa. Reporters assailed him as he walked down the gangplank, begging him to explain the theory of relativity on the spot. Einstein and his party were welcomed to New York by the mayor and the president of the New York City Council, Fiorello La Guardia. Einstein didn't talk much about the Zionist cause because he felt he did not know enough about it. But he did give many lectures about the theory of relativity in various cities, using an interpreter for fear that audiences would not understand his thick German accent.

Everywhere Einstein and Elsa went, they were accepted with open arms. He and Elsa attended a string of banquets and parties. At Princeton University he was awarded an honorary degree. Then it was on to England, to deliver more lectures about relativity. His presence there helped relations between England and Germany, so badly damaged during the First World War.

IN THEIR OWN WORDS

'Nationalism is an infantile [childish] sickness. It is the measles of the human race.'

EINSTEIN DENOUNCES NATIONALISM AS THE REASON BEHIND WAR.

ABOVE: *Einstein (centre) with fellow scientists Paul Langevin (front, third from right) and Dr Smith (to the left of Einstein), during an anti-war demonstration in Berlin, in 1923. Langevin was a French physicist who became recognized for his work on electron theory and magnetism. Like Einstein, he believed that logic could help make the world a better place. He and Einstein were good friends.*

THE NOBEL PRIZE

While touring Japan in November 1922, Einstein was told the news that he had won the 1921 Nobel Prize for Physics. The Royal Swedish Academy of Science gave him the award, not for the theories of relativity, but for his earlier work on the photoelectric effect. Since he was out of the country when the announcement was made, the award was received on his behalf by the German ambassador in Stockholm. As promised, Einstein handed the award money to Mileva.

Back in Berlin, he continued his studies into the behaviour of atoms, molecules and light. Together with the Indian scientist Satyendra Bose, Einstein did work that established the reality of photons, packets of energy from light or other forms of radiation. Then he turned his attention to explaining gravity and electromagnetism in one theory, the unification theory, which was a work he never finished.

In the evenings, Einstein and Elsa often attended banquets and dinners given in their honour by Berlin society. Einstein liked to shock people on these occasions by wearing shoes with no socks on. He let his hair grow long and unkempt.

In his spare time, the scientist played the violin, or locked himself in his study to read his beloved book. Sometimes he tinkered on the piano. Other times he would play his violin in public to help an up-and-coming concert artist. When the weather was good, Einstein used to sail his dinghy in the lakes of the River Havel just outside Berlin. Sailing was a sport he could indulge in. It meant he could get a lot of fresh air without taxing his weak heart.

On 14 March 1929, Einstein celebrated his fiftieth birthday. He received presents from all over the world. His friends suggested to the local council that he should be given a summer house near the lakes where he sailed his boat. But members of the council, who were anti-Semitic Nazis, kept objecting to the plan.

In the end, Einstein bought his own holiday home in Calputh, a village near the Havel River. His friends gave him a brand new dinghy. Life seemed to be comfortable for the Einsteins but, with the rise of Nazi power in Germany, Albert knew in his heart of hearts that there was trouble ahead.

ABOVE: *Einstein was a skilled sailor, who would go out in his boat in all weather.*

THE PHOTON

All forms of radiation, including light and X-rays, come in particles or packets of energy called photons. When you turn on a light, you create billions of photons in an instant. The photons of different-coloured lights contain different amounts of energy. Photons of blue light have twice as much energy as photons of red light.

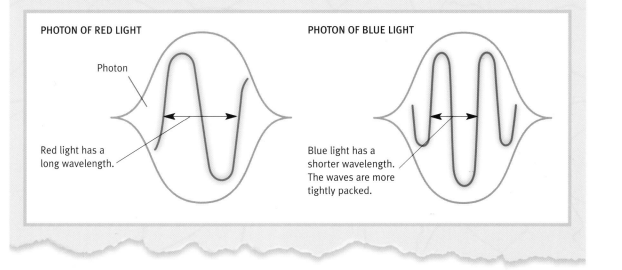

PHOTON OF RED LIGHT

Photon

Red light has a long wavelength.

PHOTON OF BLUE LIGHT

Blue light has a shorter wavelength. The waves are more tightly packed.

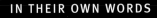

'Two things are infinite: the universe and human stupidity, and I'm not sure about the universe.'

EINSTEIN REFLECTING ON THE HUMAN CONDITION.

The Nazi Threat

IN 1930, EINSTEIN began a series of annual visits to Caltech, the California Institute of Technology in Pasadena, USA. His role was that of visiting professor, but he also found time to meet Edwin Hubble, the American astronomer who was the first to demonstrate galaxies beyond the Milky Way. In 1932, Einstein was asked to join the Institute for Advanced Studies in Princeton. The appointment meant that he would be able to divide his time between the USA and Berlin.

In January 1933, while the Einsteins were in California, Hitler was elected Chancellor of Germany. The Nazis immediately attacked the Einsteins' house in Berlin, claiming to be looking for illegal guns. They burnt copies of Einstein's books about relativity in public. German newspapers denounced the scientist as a 'Communist Jew', the worst kind of enemy Germany could have. His bank account was frozen. The German ambassador in the USA warned the Einsteins that it would be foolish and dangerous to return home.

In March of that year, the Einsteins travelled from the USA to England and then to Belgium, where they rented a house in the seaside resort of Le Coq Sur Mer. Someone gave them a Nazi document listing all Germany's enemies. Einstein was at the top of the list. Under his picture were printed the words: 'Not yet hanged'. Terrified, Elsa hired bodyguards to protect her husband.

Einstein was so angered by the Nazis that he declared he would take up arms against them to protect the rest of Europe. His words upset many pacifists, but the scientist had realized

BELOW: *While lecturing in California, Einstein often took well-deserved holidays. Here he is in Palm Springs, chatting to film director Ernst Lubitsch (left), while Elsa reclines in the background. This picture was taken in 1933, the same year that Hitler came to power in Germany.*

just how great the Nazi threat was. On 7 October 1933, shortly after giving a speech at the Albert Hall in London, the Einsteins sailed to the USA. They were never to return to Europe again.

In the USA, the Einsteins went to live in Princeton, where a friend of Albert's, called Abraham Flexner, had set up the Institute of Advanced Studies. His aim was to create a centre of study where Americans could do research that competed with the rest of the world. Flexner wanted Einstein to be on his staff because he would bring prestige to the Institute. The Einsteins moved into a comfortable house at 112 Mercer Street. There Einstein became a local celebrity.

ABOVE: *Adolf Hitler greets Nazi supporters at Nuremberg in 1933. Hitler transformed Germany from a republic to a dictatorship. His invasion of Poland in 1939 precipitated the Second World War. When the Germans lost the war, Hitler killed himself in a bunker.*

BELOW: *Einstein delivers a speech to help the cause of Jewish refugees fleeing Nazi persecution in Germany, at the Royal Albert Hall, London, on 3 October 1933.*

LIFE IN THE USA

Princeton was the perfect environment for Einstein. It was quiet. He had very little teaching to do, which left him a lot of time for study and research. A good wage meant that he and Elsa did not have any worries about money. The great scientist could get on with his work on the unification theory, in which he sought to unite gravity and electromagnetism.

However, across the Atlantic Ocean, things were different. In Germany, the Nazis were expelling anyone whose political views did not fit in with theirs. Some of these people were scientists, and they fled to the USA. Using his influence, Einstein helped find them academic posts in US universities.

In 1939, with the Second World War looming on the European horizon, it was announced that scientists had found a way to split the atom and harness nuclear energy. Much of their discovery was based on Einstein's earlier work on the atom and the theory of relativity. Leo Szilard, one of the scientists involved in the discovery, approached Einstein. He explained that the formulae for splitting the atom could be developed into making atomic bombs. Perhaps the Nazis were working on the weapons already. The President of the USA had to be warned. The USA and Britain had to start their own nuclear bomb programme, and only Einstein could convince President Roosevelt of the danger.

Einstein was horrified that anyone would want to use nuclear energy to make a bomb. He also had his doubts whether such a thing was possible. But, knowing what destruction the Nazis were capable of, he agreed to write to President Roosevelt. The President took immmediate action and work on producing the atomic bomb started the very evening he received

BELOW: *Einstein with Elsa (right) and Mrs Theresa Durlach at a dinner held to celebrate the 100th anniversary of the birth of Alfred B. Nobel, on 18 December 1933. Einstein, who won the 1921 Nobel Prize for Physics, was guest of honour at the awards, which were held in New York City. Elsa died three years later, in 1936*

'Some recent work by E. Fermi and L. Szilard, which has been communicated to me in manuscript, leads me to expect that the element uranium may be turned into a new and important source of energy in the immediate future... it may become possible to set up a nuclear chain reaction in a large mass of uranium, by which vast amounts of power and large quantities of new radium-like elements would be generated...

This new phenomenon would also lead to the construction of bombs... A single bomb of this type, carried by boat and exploded in a port, might very well destroy the whole port together with some of the surrounding territory.'

EXTRACT FROM EINSTEIN'S LETTER TO PRESIDENT ROOSEVELT, 2 AUGUST 1939, THE LETTER THAT STARTED THE ARMS RACE.

BELOW: *Franklin D. Roosevelt was President of the USA from 1933 to 1945. A popular polititian, he was elected four times. He dealt with the Great Depression of the 1930s and proved to be a great leader during the Second World War.*

the letter. Einstein, who was still completely opposed to war and violence, did not take an active part in making the bombs that destroyed Hiroshima on 6 August 1945, and Nagasaki three days later. After the war, he was to call the letter he sent to Roosevelt, 'the greatest mistake of my life'.

Final Years

IT WAS REPORTED that Einstein's reaction to the news of the atom bombs dropped on Japan was: 'Oh, horrible'. He believed that the world was poised on the brink of total destruction. After the war, the USA and Britain shared the secrets of nuclear power with France. Soon, China and Russia too had started programmes to construct the bomb.

Einstein started a campaign to stop the manufacture of atom bombs. He believed that a power as great as atomic energy had to be treated with great care. It should not be used by one country to destroy another. He explained to people that they had to change the way they viewed the world. They had to see it as one world and not a collection of countries divided by borders and hatred.

BELOW: *The city of Nagasaki on 9 August 1945, after the USA dropped an atom bomb on it. A busy port in Japan, Nagasaki had known prosperity for many years before the Second World War.*

LEFT: *Einstein and his step-daughter Margot becoming US citizens on 1 October 1940. They took their oath of allegiance in a New Jersey courtroom. Although happy to be an American, Einstein believed in the 'One World' theory, an idea that all the nations of the world could be peacefully united under one common authority.*

For the next ten years, Einstein continued working on his unification theory. Life in Princeton was peaceful. As he grew older, Einstein became a treasured part of the community. Slowly, however, he started losing his grip on life as he struggled to finish his work. Sometimes he forgot where he lived. One day he even got on a bus and gave the driver the wrong fare. The driver, unaware that he was talking to the famous Einstein, is reported to have said 'You're not very good at adding up, are you?'.

Over the years, his health deteriorated. In the spring of 1955, Einstein collapsed with a stomach complaint. Four days later he was admitted to hospital. He died peacefully at 1.15 am on 18 April. The greatest scientist of the twentieth century, the man who had changed forever the way we look at space, time and the universe, was gone.

IN THEIR OWN WORDS

'The most beautiful thing we can experience is the mysterious. It is the source of all true art and science. He to whom emotion is a stranger, who can no longer pause to wonder and stand rapt in awe, is as good as dead: his eyes are closed.'

ALBERT EINSTEIN IN 'MY CREDO', A SPEECH GIVEN TO THE GERMAN LEAGUE OF HUMAN RIGHTS IN BERLIN DURING THE AUTUMN OF 1932.

The Legacy of Einstein

ALTHOUGH EINSTEIN NEVER finished his
unification theory, where he tried to explain gravity and
electromagnetism in one package, he left a legacy of work
for other scientists to continue. He was, in fact, ahead of his
time in his thinking. Throughout the 1990s, scientists were
trying to work out a mathematical formula that would
explain all the forces and fields of physics – not just gravity
and electromagnetism – in one theory. Scientists call the
work, 'The Theory of Everything'.

Einstein's quantum theory, the idea that light is a series of
particles, or photons, each one of them a small packet of
energy, also had a profound effect on the way people looked
at creation. Before Einstein, people believed that the universe
was constant and unchanging, and that it came into being as
it is today. From Einstein's research, and that of scientists
since his death, we now know that the universe started from
one small burst of energy, which was smaller than an atom.
We call this idea the 'Big Bang Theory.'

BELOW: *A nuclear test
explosion mushrooms over
American soil in April 1954.
Shortly before he died in 1955,
Einstein and other famous
scientists signed a declaration
warning the world that atomic
bombs might destroy the world.*

'To sense that behind anything that can be experienced there is something that our mind cannot grasp and whose beauty and sublimity reaches us only indirectly and as a feeble reflection, this is religiousness.'

ALBERT EINSTEIN ON HIS BELIEFS, IN HIS SPEECH 'MY CREDO', GIVEN TO THE GERMAN LEAGUE OF HUMAN RIGHTS IN BERLIN DURING THE AUTUMN OF 1932.

Today, many scientists believe that one day the universe will spread out so much that it will collapse on itself and implode in a 'Big Crunch'. Then, they believe it will be reborn again as a small burst of energy.

Einstein's discoveries about the behaviour of electromagnetic waves also led to the invention of the laser. Today lasers are used in many ways, including hospital treatment, and the making of CD and DVD players.

Einstein's work on atoms led to the discovery of nuclear energy. Although it has been used destructively to make atom bombs, nuclear energy can also be used to help reduce environmental pollution, by taking the place of fossil fuels such as coal and oil. However, many people believe that the production of nuclear energy is too dangerous because of the risks involved when things go wrong.

As we begin the twenty-first century, people are starting to look at the world with new eyes. Thanks to Einstein, we are conscious that we are but one small part in the vast and exciting puzzle of creation. We are also aware of the harm our new-found powers can inflict on our fragile planet.

RIGHT: *A scientist conducts research on fibre-optic lasers. Light is bounced along hollow tubes the width of a human hair.*

ABOVE: *In nuclear power stations, nuclear energy is used to produce electricity. All stations have a reactor core where the energy is produced. A heat exchanger then carries the heat from the core to a water supply. The heat turns the water into steam, which powers the electricity generators.*

Timeline

1687

Sir Isaac Newton publishes his work about gravity in his book, *Philosophiae Naturalis Principia Mathematica* (Mathematical Principles of Natural Philosophy).

1772

The Swedish chemist Carl Wilhelm Scheele discovers the existence of oxygen.

1783

John Michell suggests the existence of black holes, then called 'dark stars'.

1864

The British scientist James Clark Maxwell publishes his theory of electromagnetism.

1879

14 MARCH: Albert Einstein is born in Ulm, Germany.

1881

NOVEMBER: Einstein's sister Maja is born.

1894

Einstein's family move to Munich, Germany.

1889

Einstein meets Max Talmud.

1895

German scientist Wilhelm Röntgen discovers X-rays.

1896

Antoine Becquerel discovers radioactivity. Einstein starts his course at the Federal Institute of Technology in Zurich, Switzerland.

1897

British physicist Joseph Thomson (1856–1940) discovers the electron.

1898

Marie and Pierre Curie discover radium.

1901

Einstein becomes a Swiss citizen. His first papers are published.

1902

16 JUNE: Einstein starts work at the Swiss Patent Office in Berne, Switzerland.

1903

6 JANUARY: Einstein marries Mileva Maric.
17 DECEMBER: Orville Wright flies the first aircraft.

1905

The *Annalen Der Physik* publishes Einstein's theory of relativity.

1907

Einstein has the idea that acceleration cancels out gravity. He starts work on the general theory of relativity.

1908

2 SEPTEMBER: Hermann Minkowski presents the idea of space-time to explain Einstein's theory of relativity.

1909

Einstein is appointed professor of physics at the University of Zurich. He resigns from the Patent Office.

1910

Einstein's son Eduard is born.

1911

British physicist Ernest Rutherford establishes the nuclear model of the atom.

1912

Austrian physicist Victor F. Hess discovers cosmic rays.

1913

Charles Fabry discovers the ozone layer.

1914

Einstein becomes a professor at the University of Berlin.
First World War begins.

1915

NOVEMBER: Einstein presents his general theory of relativity to the Prussian Academy of Science in Berlin.

1918

First World War ends.

1919

FEBRUARY: Einstein divorces Mileva.
29 MAY: Arthur Eddington takes photographs of the total eclipse of the Sun, in Principe.
JUNE: Einstein marries Elsa Lowenthal.
6 NOVEMBER: Eddington shows his findings to the Royal Society and the Royal Astronomical Society in London.

1920

Einstein joins the Zionist movement.

1921

Einstein wins the Nobel Prize for Physics.

1933

Adolf Hitler becomes Chancellor in Germany.
3 OCTOBER: Einstein makes his last public appearance in Europe, at the Royal Albert Hall in London. He gives a speech to help the cause of Jewish refugees fleeing Nazi persecution in Germany. Shortly afterwards he leaves for the USA, never to return home to Germany.

1934

Hitler assumes the title *Fuhrer und Reichskanzler* (leader and reich chancellor), the undisputed leader of Germany.

1936

DECEMBER: Elsa Einstein dies.

1939

Second World War begins.
2 AUGUST: Einstein signs a letter to President Roosevelt, urging him to look into the possibility of making an atom bomb.

1945

7 MAY: Second World War comes to an end in Europe.
6 AUGUST: An atom bomb is dropped on Hiroshima, in Japan.
9 AUGUST: An atom bomb is dropped on Nagasaki, also in Japan.
14 AUGUST: Japan surrenders to the Allies, bringing the Second World War to an end in the Pacific.

1948

Chaim Weizmann becomes the first president of the newly created country of Israel.

1952

Einstein's health starts to deteriorate.

1955

18 APRIL: Einstein dies at the age of seventy-six.
Dr Narinder Kapany of Imperial College, London, shows that light can travel along a fine fibre made of two different types of glass.

1958

American surgeon Basil Hirschowitz uses an endoscope for the first time.

1966

Scientists Charles Kao and George Hockham prove that fibre optics can be used to carry telecommunications signals.

Glossary

Academic
Something or someone that belongs to a place of learning.

Acceleration
Gaining speed.

Algebra
A branch of mathematics that uses letters and numbers to show relations between quantities.

Anti-semitic
Dislike or hatred of Jews.

Astronomical
Related to astronomy, the scientific study of objects beyond the Earth.

Counter-manifesto
A document that opposes a manifesto.

Equations
Mathematical formulae that make two quantities equal.

Electro-magnetism
Magnetism produced by a current of electricity.

Formula
A set of rules.

Gravity
The force that makes stones fall to the ground, keeps the Moon orbiting the Earth and the planets orbiting the Sun.

Individuality
Characteristics that make a person or object different from others.

Kosher
Food prepared according to the laws of the Jewish religion.

Manifesto
A document stating the beliefs of a group of people, usually a political party.

Mass
Matter without any shape.

Matter
Something solid.

Military duty
Serving in the army, navy or air force.

Molecules
Very small particles made up of two atoms held together by a chemical bond.

Nobel Prize
The Nobel Prize was the idea of the Swedish chemist, Alfred B. Nobel (1833–96). Founded in 1901, the prize is awarded to people who have made outstanding contributions in the fields of physics, chemistry, medicine, literature, world peace and economics.

Pacifist
Someone who refuses to be violent or support violence.

Patent
An official document that registers an idea as someone's property.

Ph.D.
An abbreviation for the qualification of Doctor of Philosophy.

Radiations
The process of giving out light, heat, electricity or other energy.

Relativity
The principle that it makes no sense to state that an object moves, except in relation to another object.

Theory
An explanation based on thought, observation and reasoning.

Thesis
An essay or written report.

Total eclipse
A total eclipse occurs when one object in space is completely hidden by another, such as a star, moon or planet.

Velocity
Speed.

Further Information

BOOKS FOR YOUNGER READERS

The Big Idea: Einstein and Relativity
by Paul Strathern (Arrow, 1997)

The Cosmic Professor: The Story of Albert Einstein
by Andrew Donkin (Hodder Wayland, 1997)

Eyewitness Science: Time and Space
by Mary and John Gribbin
(Dorling Kindersley, 1994)

Famous People: Albert Einstein
by Ibi Lepscky and Paolo Cardoni
(Barron's Educational, 1992)

Groundbreakers: Einstein
by Struan Reid
(Heinemann, 2001)

Livewire Real Lives: Einstein
by Mike Alcott (Hodder & Stoughton
Educational, 2000)

The World in the Time of Albert Einstein
by Fiona Macdonald (Belitha Press, 1998)

BOOKS FOR OLDER READERS

Einstein, A Life In Science
by Michael White and John Gribbin
(Pocket Books, 1997)

The World As I See It
by Albert Einstein (John Lane, 1935)

Out Of My Later Years
by Albert Einstein (Thames & Hudson, 1950)

WEBSITES

There are many websites dedicated to Albert Einstein. Here are just a few to start with:

Einstein: Person of the Century
www.westegg.com/einstein/
Good information about the greatest scientist of the twentieth century. Includes links, pictures and biographical notes.

Einstein for Kids
sites.huji.ac.il/jnul/einstein/.index6
Maintained by the Hebrew University in Israel, this site provides a humorous look at Einstein, as well as links, a list of books to read and pictures to download.

Einstein's Wisdom
http://www.ludwig.ucl.ac.uk/st/einst.html
A collection of quotes by Einstein.

Einstein Revealed
http://www.pbs.org/wgbh/nova/einstein/
Lots of information about Einstein. Includes a brief timeline of his life and a time-travel game.

Index

Page numbers in **bold** are pages where there is a photograph or an illustration.